Poems of Hope
and Humor

Poems of Hope and Humor

Elaine Bishop

authorHOUSE®

AuthorHouse™ LLC
1663 Liberty Drive
Bloomington, IN 47403
www.authorhouse.com
Phone: 1-800-839-8640

Published by AuthorHouse   10/07/2013

ISBN: 978-1-4918-2190-9 (sc)
ISBN: 978-1-4918-2191-6 (e)

Library of Congress Control Number: 2013917736

CONTENTS

HUMOR

A Birthday Toast 3
A Trip To The Grocery Store 4
House Wives Lament.. 5
A Fun Day.. 6
Putting On My Shoes 7
Laughter Is Good For You 8
Seeing Spots 9
Square Dance Club 10
The Storm That Went Out To Sea 12
Those Golden Years 13
Winter Snow...14

EASTER

Easter 17
Glorious Easter 18
Happy Angels..19
Victory..20

HOPE AND INSPIRATION

A Summer Day 25
Abortion...26
Commissioned...27
Communion 28
Each Day..29

Find Time To Pray 30

Tragedy And Horror 31

God Changes Lives 32

Does God Care? 33

Gods' Army 34

He Never Left Your Side.......................................35

Humility...36

A Golden Sunset..37

Honor And Glory 38

Imagine 39

Joy In Serving Jesus 40

Keep Your Eyes On Jesus 41

Lord I Want To Serve You 42

Morning Coffee 43

My Legacy..44

Praises To God 45

Sing A Song 46

Sitting At The Feet Of Jesus 47

Step Out In Faith...48

There Sits A Lad Alone In Jail.................................49

CHRISTMAS

A Cold Night In Bethlehem 53

A Manger Scene Upon My Door................................54

Christmas Is Fast Approaching.................................55

Merry Christmas 56

Christ's Birth..57

In Bethlehem...58

No Room...59

HUMOR

A Birthday Toast

We know we're getting older when our hair begins to thin,

Can't remember what we came for, in the room we find we're in.

The cupboards seem much higher than they ever were before,

And we have to get back up at night, forgot to lock the door,

There are aches and pains all over and it really does feel bad,

It's strange they come in places that we never knew we had

We have lots of medications, choose capsule, pill or rub

No room in our cupboard so we store them in our tub,

Please don't be discouraged as you join our aging crowd,

If you cannot hear us, turn your hearing aid to loud,

So enjoy this brand new life style you are starting here this year,

Dear friend we raise our glasses for a toast to health and cheer.

A Trip To The Grocery Store

I'm leaving the house for a trip to the store,

I've got my shopping bags galore,

All my coupons in an envelope,

Of using them, I have great hope,

Silver coins in a special purse

Can this truly get much worse?

My shopping card I have in hand,

To use for bargains yet unplanned,

If I have to take much more,

I'll never make it out the door

Check my bag for some extra cash,

To my car I must make a dash,

I'm so tired I start to snore,

So much, for my trip to the grocery store.

House Wives Lament

All you pesky salesmen,
Won't you leave me alone?
If you're not on my doorstep,
You're surely on my phone,
I've got encyclopedias,
And all the magazines,
Lots of your free samples,
Not worth a row of beans,
I've seen all your new gadgets,
And all your brushes too,
There's nothing that the Five and Ten,
Won't sell for less than you,
My house has just been painted,
Don't need your shiny tin,
So get your foot out of my door,
'Cause you're not getting in.

A Fun Day

I have to go to the Lab today to have some blood work done,

I'm sure you know the feeling it really is no fun,

First you have to register, your life's story you must tell,

Insurance cards and date of birth, it makes me want to yell,

Then, they make you take a cup and in it, try to pee,

They make you do it on demand it never works for me,

Then here comes the needle, a vein needs to be found,

Every time I go there, there's none of them around,

Finally they find one and take out what they need,

For all the holes they make in me I try to pay no heed,

I'm sure when I get home again these memories will fade,

For all my troubles all I get is one huge, pink, band aid.

Putting On My Shoes

I tried to put my shoes on so carefully today,

But, found my swollen kneecaps kept getting in the way,

I had to opt for slippers though stylish they were not,

And really could not walk in them I had to kind of trot.

I had to pick up something that had fallen on the floor,

And found my poor old aching back was oh, so very sore,

I tried to thread a needle, needed glasses now I found,

Then dropped that darn old needle, had to leave it on the ground.

I used to sew and bake my bread with fingers, oh so nimble,

Remember all the clothes I made and didn't need a thimble.

In spite of all these problems, I thank God for each new day,

For I am learning patience in His own time and way.

Laughter Is Good For You

Don't be afraid of laughter,
A laugh is good for you,
It may not end your troubles,
Or save your bursting bubbles,
But, it gives new perspective to,
The things that really bother you,
And maybe help you set things straight,
And realize how very great,
Our heavenly Father, who loves us so,
Will let laughter mend, that heart of woe,
So laugh when things are going wrong,
It shows your love for God is strong,
So encourage others to laugh with you,
For God has sent His love to you.

Seeing Spots

When I woke up this morning I found another spot
I do not know what's causing them, but I sure have a lot.
Grandma called them liver spots that does not appeal to me,
Now I'm hearing age spots, oh Lord, that could not be,
I'd pass them off as freckles but that would not be true,
And I must always tell the truth whatever else I do,
As long as I've no name for them and I'm still in the dark,
I've decided I'll call them, my special beauty mark.

Square Dance Club

I thought when I got older,

I would join a square dance club,

A "friend" so kind invited me,

But, now here comes the rub,

I knew I owned just one left foot

I know I've proved that's true,

But, now I've found to my chagrine,

I've not one but two,

While trying to learn the grand square,

I learned it in reverse,

That's the step that I took, no time to rehearse,

The gracious caller, his name is Ed,

Is really quite a clown,

But, if you make a bad mistake,

He never puts you down,

My new friends here, I'd hoped to keep,

This next step makes me sigh,

For Ed stands there and tells us,

We must trade or pass them by,

The choir next door is recruiting,

New members along the way,

And the way my dancing's going,

That looks better every day

The Storm That Went Out To Sea

Friday at choir I was told,

The storm's gone out to sea,

The fact that it was snowing out,

Was not to bother me,

So I went home and went to bed,

With happy thoughts within my head,

Of swimming pools and ice cold tea,

Because the storm had gone out to sea,

When I woke up and opened my eyes,

I couldn't believe the funny surprise,

Ten foot drifts as tall as a tree

Dumped by the storm that went out to sea,

The dog got buried in an avalanche

While doing his job 'neath a snowy branch,

I could not even find my car

Without a compass and the old north star,

WHEN THE WEATHERMAN SAYS GONE OUT TO SEA,

TAKE IT WITH A GRAIN OF SALT, LIKE ME.

Those Golden Years

I'm finding out those golden years aren't all they're cracked up to be,
They really are quite rusty if you are asking me
My knees don't seem to want to bend so I can kneel to pray,
I know that God still hears me each and every day.
Picking up the things I drop which is, more often now,
I know I have to pick them up I just don't know, quite how
The things I use to do with ease are a challenge every day,
All the strength I used to have, has faded all away,
Finding new ways of doing things can be a lot of fun
Of course, the old way was the best for getting things all done,
I have given up the fight for wearing panty hose
They really do not get along with my arthritic toes.
I really feel accomplished when I am fully dressed,
And everything is in its place, I've been truly blest.
I still am very grateful for the years God's given me,
He's right there to help you too, just ask Him and you'll see.

Winter Snow

There's snow piled high upon my car and freezing rain beside,
I know that I must move my car but I'd rather be inside,
It's really getting slippery and when I went out to scrape
I wished I had a balmy isle to which I could escape
I'm sure we are in need of snow to fill our lakes and rivers,
I just wish that it could come without the freezing shivers
So I'll just stay inside the house where I am toasty warm,
And hope that all the other folks survive this winter storm.

EASTER

Easter

Those joyous Hosannas of Sunday, have all been silenced now,
And a sinless man has been betrayed and put on trial some how
He has suffered crucifixion on a cruel and painful cross,
The world seems unaware it has suffered a great loss,
His body placed within a tomb of cold unyielding stone
The doorway sealed he's laid to rest in that cold room alone,
But, early Sunday morning, a new day has been born,
For Christ our Savior is alive, this glorious Easter Morn,
By resurrection he has conquered death and sin and shame,
Eternal life he has given us, so praise His Holy Name.

Glorious Easter

The sky was dark and cold and gray,
As soldiers led our Lord away,
Up Calvary's hill, through jeering crowd,
Beneath the cross His head was bowed,

Behold! Three crosses on the hill,
His cry "'tis finished" lingers still,
From borrowed stable to borrowed tomb,
It seems for Christ there was no room,

But wait! A glorious day is born,
OUR LORD IS RISEN THIS EASTER MORN,
He's conquered sin and death and pain,
He lives forever, our King to reign.

Happy Angels

How happy the Angels must have been on that first Easter Morn,

They'd been watching over Christ since the day that He was born,

They'd seen Him in the temple when He was just a boy,

Seeing Him do His fathers' will, filled their hearts with joy,

The time of His Baptism and His ministry begun,

They'd watched Him oh, so carefully, This Man, Gods' only son.

They saw Him choose disciples to learn, from Him each day,

Trying to be more like Him as they followed in His way,

They were there when he blessed the lunch of a small boys' fish and bread,

And saw the amazement of the crowd when they had all been fed,

The healing of the sick and blind they saw all of this too,

They were pleased at all the things that He could say and do,

They saw Him in Gethsemane in pain and agony,

Willing to do His fathers' will whatever the cost would be

Through His resurrection the battle now is done,

Happy were the angels for the VICTORY HAD BEEN WON!

Victory

Beneath a knarled old olive tree,

The Savior kneels to weep,

As not far off his closest friends,

Have fallen off to sleep.

Hear the prayer, oh, Father God,

Of this your only son,

I would this cup could pass from me,

But, let Your will be done.

The soldiers come and take this man,

A prisoner away,

Chained up between the soldiers,

It is almost break of day.

Shackled now both hand and foot,

He stands in Pilates' hall,

This sinless one stands calmly by,

Condemned to die for all,

Up Calverys hill with thorn crowned brow,

He falls beneath the load,

Now filled with love for all,

He stumbles up that road.

Nailed in pain upon this cross,

"'tis finished" is His cry,
This very Son of God has died,
To save both you and I.
The first day of the week has come,
Sad friends walk toward the tomb,
Wondering how to roll the stone,
That sealed that ugly room!
But, Angels greet their wondering eyes,
With message, oh, so sweet,
He is not here He's risen!
Quickly go, this news repeat,
And so this message through the years,
Still frees man from sins' prison,
And echoes joyfully again,
HE IS NOT HERE! HE'S RISEN!

HOPE AND INSPIRATION

A Summer Day

There's nothing like a summer day,

To help to chase the blues away,

The songs of birds up in the trees,

The flight of butterflies and bees,

Flowers in bloom in garden fair,

A whisper of lilac in the air,

The happy sound of gurgling brook,

A pleasant place to read a book,

The sound of children's playful laughter,

Lingering on the air long after,

Setting sun has cooled the day,

And they have each gone on their way,

There's nothing like a summer day,

To help to chase the blues away.

Abortion

Don't you hear a baby crying in the distance, everyday?

For the life that might have been that abortion took away,

Don't you hear a baby crying for the Mom he'll never know?

For all the things he could have done if he'd been let to grow,

Don't you hear a baby crying for the Doctors' cruel and still,

Who seem to think that it's alright to murder and to kill?

Don't you hear a baby crying for the women everywhere?

Who've lost Gods' gift of loving for the children they should bear,

Don't you hear a baby crying, OH GOD, please hear my prayer!

And bring abortion to an end here and everywhere.

Commissioned

Let's not leave it to the Pastor, when we see there's work to do,

He's not the only one commissioned, don't forget that we were too,

We may not have a license hanging on our wall,

But we can tell to others that Jesus died for all,

A visit to a shut in, who is lonely, sad and blue,

Not only brings them comfort but will bring true joy to you,

A kind and loving word of cheer, to a lonely little child,

Will show the love of Jesus, so tender, meek and mild,

Perhaps a homeless person who longs for love so much,

Will find it when we greet them, with a kindly, loving touch,

It may be your neighbor, or a friend out on the street,

So greet them with a loving smile, when you chance to meet,

So don't leave it to the Pastor when there's some work to do,

And prove we've not forgotten we were commissioned too.

Communion

Are you taking communion on Sunday while sitting across the aisle?

From a lady you think is too pious, so you won't even give her a smile?

Are you taking communion on Sunday sitting smugly in you pew?

Ignoring that lonely teenager, who only needs friendship from you?

Are you taking communion on Sunday while sitting directly behind?

That man whose harsh words upset you forgiveness from you will he find?

Are you taking communion on Sunday with a heart filled only with strife?

Forgetting the emblems before you, represents Christ's giving His life?

To save the afore mentioned people sitting in every pew,

Please try to remember, my dear one, He gave His life for them and for you!

Each Day

God makes every day,
No matter what the date,
So, let's live each one carefully,
With lots of love not hate,
Remembering to thank Him,
For blessings great and small,
For God is the author of them all,
Perhaps, someone has smiled your way,
Or said a cheery word,
They might have been the only ones,
That day, you may have heard,
For, God can send you greetings,
And blessings quite unknown,
Sometimes sent through others
His love for you is shown,
So keep right on trusting Him,
And praying all the way,
His blessings will be sent to you,
Each and every day!

Find Time To Pray

Sometimes I get up quickly to start my busy day,

My life gets so entangled I don't take time to pray,

It seems I have forgotten all the lord has done for me,

I know that he is helping me be all that I can be,

Later on throughout the day my problems seem so large,

Then suddenly I remember, I have not let him take charge,

I quickly say I'm sorry lord, for not including you,

In all the things I have to say and all the things I do,

At that point my savior, starts to brighten up my day,

It seems that all my worries have quickly gone away,

Now I try to remember if my day's to work out fair,

To start each morning early,

With a sweet, sweet time of prayer.

Tragedy And Horror

For tragedy and horror
We try to set the blame,
And never look inside ourselves,
Or bow our heads in shame,
We try some stricter gun laws,
Less violence on T. V.
Or blame the teachers in our schools,
For thinking passively,
Though all these things contribute,
And truly play a part,
The thing that's really needed,
Is a change within our heart,
So we don't say and do cruel things,
That really hurt each other,
Or cause such pain and sadness
We make outcasts of our brother,
God alone can make these changes,
In the heart of every one,
And that's through true repentance,
And belief in Christ, Gods' Son.

God Changes Lives

I tried so hard to change my life to what it ought

To be,

I worked and worked so very hard to see a change

In me,

I tried everything I knew, and all that I could

Do,

To make myself all over and make my life

Anew,

Until I realized only God can change the inner

Man,

The only way that I can change is by living by Gods'

Plan,

He may not change me right away, a quickly as I

Would,

Some lessons I may need to learn for my own very

Good,

So listen well, and from all this a lesson may be

Learned,

In His own time our lives will change, a change for which we've

Yearned.

Does God Care?

God does not care about folks, color, race or creed,

He loves them all and tells them He can meet their need,

We all are individuals with the capacity to love,

And that's exactly what God sends down from up above,

When we believe in Jesus and ask Him to come in,

The Holy Spirit comes to help us, stay away from sin,

That does not mean we'll never sin, but now we have the power,

To grow in the Spirit day by day, even hour by hour,

So open up your heart and let Christ's Spirit take control,

Of every little part of your body and your soul,

Rest in Him completely and your future is secure,

Let him help you stay away from worldly sins allure.

Gods' Army

We're all in Gods' army,

Whether short or tall,

Recruited by our savior,

Who died for one and all,

We may not hold prestigious rank,

Or skills beyond compare,

But go where Jesus sends you,

He will meet you there,

Our duty may be as simple,

As sending up a prayer,

But, our commander Jesus,

Will keep you in his care

So take your marching orders,

And follow his command

We already have the victory,

Held in his holy hand

He Never Left Your Side

You may have trials and troubles,

That you think are yours alone,

But, if you look around you,

Others troubles you'll be shown,

God is with you always,

And knows your grief and pain,

Someday you'll understand it all,

Those trials were for your gain,

To help you trust in him alone,

As comfort, friend and guide,

You'll know when looking back, on things,

He never left your side.

Humility

God please keep us humble,

Keep us from prides' sinful way,

Help us to remember

To rely on You each day,

Don't let us place, our confidence

In things we say and do,

But help us to remember,

All blessings come from you.

Please, God, keep us humble,

As we bow before Your throne,

Knowing all praise and glory,

Are Yours and Yours alone.

A Golden Sunset

I saw a gorgeous sunset as I took a ride today,

All golden hues of pinks and blues and a few clouds colored gray,

The Master painter must a have used a many colored brush,

To make that golden sunset and He did not seem to rush,

It did not last a long, long time before it slipped away,

But in my memory, of that day, it's truly going to stay.

Honor And Glory

If there is honor and glory to be given,

Let it go to Jesus who died,

For without his shed blood we'd be nothing,

We'd only be puffed up with pride,

All glory to God through Christ Jesus,

Who's been raised and is coming again,

Send up your praise and thanksgiving

Knowing we'll see him then.

Scripture: "GOD RESISETH THE PROUD BUT GIVETH
GRACE TO THE HUMBLE."

Imagine

Imagine a world without any pain,
No fighting and strife for worldly gain,
A place where peace and quiet reign,
No need for a walker, crutch or cane,
God is preparing a place like that,
He's laying out the welcome mat,
For all who believe on His only Son,
Sent to save us, everyone,
Through His death on Calvary,
Won't you answer His earnest plea?
Of sinner, won't you come to me?
Open your heart and let Him come in,
He will save your soul from sin,
When He comes back He'll welcome you,
Because you believed His word is true.

Joy In Serving Jesus

There is joy in serving Jesus,

As we travel on lifes' road,

There is joy in serving Jesus

Knowing He will share our load,

Just remember all His promises,

To each one he'll be true,

It won't be Long, before you see Him,

Coming back for you,

Oh, there is joy in serving Jesus,

Keep his love within your heart,

There is joy in serving Jesus

His grace and peace He will impart,

There's still much work needs doing,

And so little time each day,

But, there is joy in serving Jesus,

All the way,

Yes, there is joy in serving Jesus,

All the way.

Keep Your Eyes On Jesus

Keep your eyes on Jesus,
As you travel on lifes' road,
Knowing He will walk with you
And share your heavy load,
Don't look away a moment,
Keep your eyes, steadfastly fixed,
On Jesus, as He leads you,
His signals won't be mixed.
He has walked this path before you,
So He surely knows the way,
So keep your eyes on Jesus,
And you will not go astray.

Lord I Want To Serve You

Lord, I want to serve you,

In any way I can,

Help me to listen your voice,

And not the voice of man

Set my feet awalking,

On the chosen path for me,

Making sure it is the path,

Where you would have me be,

Though enemies surround me,

And threaten all the way,

'Tis you, oh Lord, I'll follow

And do everything you say.

So make your message plain to me

Make sure I understand,

Exactly what I am to do,

Kept in your loving hand.

Morning Coffee

I have my morning coffee, every day, with my best friend,

We have so much to talk about it seems there is no end,

Sometimes we talk of politics and the leaders of our nation

We speak of getting back again to the God of our foundation,

He tells me of His sadness for the condition that we're in,

I ask that He will help us to turn our back on sin,

He reminds me of the many lives that abortion has cut short,

Because of rash decisions made within our nations court,

We talk about our service men and all the women too,

I ask that He will help, to bring them safely through,

We speak about the violence, of which He's much aware,

Of all the grief that this has brought He hears it all in prayer,

I ask Him please to tell me just what it's going to take,

To bring our nation back again, we need to be awake,

We Christian brothers need to bow, in truly HUMBLE PRAYER,

SEEK HIS FACE, TURN OUR BACK ON SIN, THEN HE
WILL HEAR UP THERE

Because He holds the universe within His mighty hand,

He promises, if we do these things, then He will heal our land.

43

My Legacy

I do not want a monument of marble, clay or stone,
Standing in a graveyard, abandoned and alone,
I want to be remembered for the kindness I have shown,
A helping hand extended to the folks that I have known,
Remembered by a little child I made to laugh with glee,
This is what I truly want, my legacy to be,
Perhaps a word of caring to a friend, who's much in need,
Remembering Christ's example in thought and word and deed,
So when my time has come and I've had to depart,
Please keep my legacy alive deep within your heart,
This is the kind of monument that lives on when we've passed,
It is the only kind you'll find, that will truly, truly last.

Praises To God

God wants us to praise him,

With anything at hand,

Harps and drums and bugles,

Praise him throughout the land,

Raise our voices ever high,

Sing songs both old and new,

Let him hear our praises,

Whatever else we do

Send this message upward,

We worship and adore you,

Never let us cease to bring,

Our praise to God anew.

Sing A Song

When your day seems dark and dreary,
And your soul is sad and weary,
Sing a song
When your path is filled with sorrow,
And you can not face tomorrow,
Sing a song
When your friends have let you down,
Don't just sit around and frown,
Sing a song
When it reaches to Gods' ear,
He will come so very near.
So, sing a song.

Sitting At The Feet Of Jesus

Don't we need to be like Mary?

And sit at Jesus feet?

But, we're so much like Martha,

Each job we must complete,

But, oh, the peace of heart and mind,

That Mary must have felt,

As lovingly at Jesus feet,

She often calmly knelt,

There are times to be like Martha,

To get work quickly done,

But, oh to be like Mary,

And learn from Gods' own son.

Step Out In Faith

When you think of the stories of Peter,
Which one do you remember the best?
I remember the story of Peter
When his faith was put to the test,
While trying to walk on the water,
He hardly had time to blink,
He took his eyes off the Master,
And suddenly started to sink,
We think as the disciples before us,
Foolish Peter impulsive and strong,
We'd never do anything so daring,
We might even think it was wrong,
But, if you think that his faith was so shallow,
It would hardly keep him afloat,
Remember my dear christian brother
He's the one who got out of the boat!

There Sits A Lad Alone In Jail

There sits a lad alone in jail,

With no one to come and pay his bail,

He'd thought that drugs were really cool,

Back in the days when he went to school,

His "friends" had promised a lot of fun,

Popularity with every one,

For a time it did prove true,

And just a joint would see him through,

'Til he let heroin and crack,

Become the monkey on his back,

He started to steal in order to pay,

For the fix he needed every day,

His parents who loved him tried their best,

To help clean up the life that he had messed,

But, nothing worked to help this boy,

Who once had been their pride and joy

On the street he finally found,

No one wanted him around,

And now he sits in a lonely jail,

With no one to come and pay his bail

There sits a lad alone in jail,

With no one to come and pay his bail,

But, suddenly he hears a voice,

"My son, you truly have a choice,

For I have come to set you free,

By my death on Calvary,

But, it's up to you what you will choose,

A life with Christ, or drugs or booze,

My life I gave your debt to pay,

But, you must choose this very day,

Upon his knees this lonely lad,

Confessed all the things he had done so bad,

Asked forgiveness for all he'd done,

And knew forgiveness from Gods' own Son,

There he sits in a lonely jail.

But, Christ has come to pay his bail,

CHRISTMAS

A Cold Night In Bethlehem

The night was cold and dark and still, as shepherds sat upon the hill,

Watching over their flocks by night, staying warm by fireside bright,

When suddenly to their surprise, appeared before their
wondering eyes,

An angel with a message bringing, joined by a choir of angels singing,

Goodwill to men and peace on earth, they told of Jesus' humble birth,

To Bethlehem, the shepherds went, to find the Babe that was
Heaven sent,

And in a stable dark and bare, they found the Child in a manger there,

They worshipped Him on bended knee, this Savior sent to set
men free,

This Christmas time should we do less, than truly bow in humbleness?

Before the King upon His throne, who died to claim His very own?

Then we can join that angel throng, in singing that first
Christmas song,

Which, echoes through the earth again, of peace on earth,
goodwill to men

A Manger Scene Upon My Door

This year I went shopping at my favorite discount store,

Looking for a manger scene to place upon my door,

To remind all those who enter of our Saviors' Holy Birth

Welcomed by the shepherds when He came down to earth,

So I started down the Christmas aisle, filled with Santa and his elves,

I found a lot of reindeer and snow men on the shelves,

Next aisle Christmas stockings and gift wrap all around

But, not a single manger in that store, could there be found.

So I went home and went to bed and tried to get some sleep,

But, my heart was very sad and I started in to weep

Because Jesus came to save us from all our guilt and sin,

But, just like Bethlehem of old, there's no room in the inn.

Jesus Christ will save you if you only ask Him to,

He'll come in and clean your heart and make your life anew,

So you see the best solution, was right there at the start

And, that's to ask the Christ Child to come live within your heart.

Christmas Is Fast Approaching

Christmas is fast approaching with its glisten and its glamour,

And all its shopping and its rushing, making lots of clamor,

I like to think that somewhere, if we really try to hear,

We'll still know the angels song, as it falls upon our ear,

For there in Bethlehem was born, in stable oh, so bare,

The Savior of the world who came, His Fathers love to share,

With shepherds there to worship midst the cattle in their stall,

God gave His Son, the greatest gift, He gave to one and all,

So this year, when you make your list, of gifts you decide upon,

Sharing Jesus should be first, help the story of His grace live on,

For that's the very greatest gift that you can ever pass along,

For in so doing you will find your faith has grown so strong.

Merry Christmas

Merry Christmas ooh, what did I say,

Did I offend someone today?

With a greeting that was only meant to remind,

That wise men, still seek and hope to find,

The Christ Child who came to save one and all,

Born in Bethlehem's stable stall,

Came through such a humble birth

The Son of God came down to earth,

The shepherds heard the angels' song,

Left their sheep and hurried along,

To find and worship that precious Child,

In a manger so meek and mild,

I think we need reminders, of that night so long ago,

How the stars shone so bright and angels came so low,

To remind us of our Glorious King,

Who came, our salvation, to bring!

I may not be politically correct.

And my reminder may be too direct,

But as long as I've breath, to worship my King,

This reminder I will faithfully bring,

MERRY CHRISTMAS!

Christ's Birth

In a manger dark and lowly,
Lay the Savior pure and holy,
Up above the angels sang,
Voices raised and heavens rang,
Across the land on that dark night,
The message spread of Godly light,
The Savior of the world was born,
Upon that early Christmas morn,
Now, let us, make the heavens ring,
And lift our voices loud and sing,
This ageless news to quickly spread,
About the child in a manger bed,
Who brought salvation, full and free,
By his death on Calvary,
For all the world to know today,
For us he gave his life away.

In Bethlehem

In the little town of Bethlehem there is a baby's cry
And awestruck shepherds in the field see angels in the sky,
In a lowly stable there the Son Of God is born,
Bringing love, and joy and peace that first Christmas morn,
This precious child grows stronger each and every day,
Showing only kindness and wisdom on the way,
Working hard with Joseph to learn a carpenters' trade,
Knowing someday by a friend that He would be betrayed,
As he grew to manhood His disciples He did choose,
As he called each one of them no one did refuse,
After three years of sharing He had to make them see
That His life would have to end on the cross of Calvary
This Christmas let's remember that Bethlehem baby's cry,
It foretold that the Son of God had to come to earth to die,
For all the sins of all mankind were laid upon Him there
We remember where He started in a lowly stable bare,
Remember as we hear all the bells of Christmas ring
It's not a babe we worship but our risen Heavenly King
Who sits upon a glorious throne and sends us Christmas love,
And wants to be remembered, as He smiles down from above.

No Room

There was no room in the inn that night,

For that tired, weary pair,

The only refuge that they found,

Was in a stable bare,

During the night a child was born,

And placed in a manger of hay,

That was the Christ Childs' humble bed,

On that first Christmas day,

The shepherds came to worship Him

In wonder and in awe,

And told of angels in the sky

And all they heard and saw,

This year, will Jesus find no room?

Just as He did before

Or will we quickly welcome Him

And open up the door,

For Jesus died for everyone,

And, by faith, we are set apart,

He only thing He really wants,

Is room within our heart.